Christie in Love

Heads

The Education of Skinny Spew

HOWARD
BRENTON

First published in Great Britain 1970
by Methuen & Co Ltd
11 New Fetter Lane, London EC4
Copyright © 1970 by Howard Brenton
SBN 416 08410 9

OOO 221 22

16268

Methuen Playscripts

The Methuen Playscripts series exists
to extend the range of plays in print by
publishing work which is not yet widely
known but which has already earned a

:h

s part

ton
f a

ye
uine,
st
on—

rial
re

By the same author
REVENGE

OTHER METHUEN PLAYSCRIPTS

CONTENTS

To Jane

Christie in Love

CHRISTIE's first appearance is in the Dracula tradition.
Happy horror, creeps and treats. He rises from the grave
luridly, in a frightening mask. It looks as if a juicy
evening's underway, all laughs, nice shivers, easy oohs
and aahs.

But that's smashed up. The lights are slammed on, and
the mask is seen as only a tatty bit of papier mâché. Off it
comes, and what's left is a feeble, ordinary man blinking
through his pebble glasses.

The Publishers asked for a production note, and I'm setting
down the devices I tried to use in the show. That's the
basic one. A kind of dislocation, tearing one style up for
another, so the proceedings lurch and all interpretations
are blocked, and the spectator hunting for an easy meaning
wearies, and is left only with CHRISTIE and his act of
love.

The play is a black sketch if played fast, and I suppose it
would be quite funny if done at that pace. But I categorically
forbid anyone to do so. I want it to last nearly an hour. It
is written to be played very slowly.

Any director who's nervous about this slowness, please
look at the first scene. David Hare, in the Portable Theatre
production, got it right and it was taking at least twenty
minutes to play. Its an old trick after all, to play the first
scene of a slow play very slowly. Once the first scene is
established, the actors can make judgements about the pauses
and little rushes needed for the interrogation scenes.

The 'Garden' is a pen, ten feet by six feet. Its sides are
two and a half feet high, and made of chicken wire. It's brim
full of torn and screwed up pages of a popular newspaper.
The spectators sit all around, and very close – there's
barely enough room for the actors to walk round the sides.
The pen is a filthy sight. The chicken wire is rusty, the
wood is stained, the paper is full of dust. It's used as
CHRISTIE's garden, his front room, a room in a police
station, an executioner's shed, a lime pit. But it's not a
'Setting' in a conventional sense. I don't want it to be <u>like</u>
a garden, or a room. It's theatrical machine, a thing you'd
only see in a show. Its a trap, a flypaper for the attention

of the spectators to stick on.

The doll is a little larger than life size. She must not be in
any way a pornographic object. She is dressed in a faded
blue skirt and dirty white blouse of the early fifties, her
skin is grey, her hair frizzy and short the   way they wore
it then. Her underwear is massive, unfrilly, not sexy. The
CONSTABLE has to undress her – that scene's tricky and he
must be able to strip her quickly. Valcro can be used instead
of buttons and eyes.

The CONSTABLE and the INSPECTOR are not 'characters',
apart from the facts of age and rank. (The INSPECTOR is
in his mid–thirties, the CONSTABLE in his late twenties.)
They are stage coppers. But they have 'sudden lights',
unpredictable speeches beyond the confines of pastiche. As
if a cardboard black and white cut–out suddenly reaches out
a fully fleshed, real hand. It's a bathos technique (the end of
HEADS works by it.) It is very cruel.

The artifice of the garden and the 'stage' nature of the
policemen's parts are intended to throw the CHRISTIE part
into relief. With CHRISTIE I tried to write a fully fledged
naturalistic part.

I am greatly indebted to William Hoyland's playing of
CHRISTIE. That the part is in a style radically different
from that of the policemen is a fundamental dislocation in
the play. Bill got it right. Over fifty performances with the
Portable Theatre, in all kinds of conditions, he developed
the part until it had an illusory effect. An obscene insolence
– in the middle of all that artificial invention, all that tat, the
garden, the doll, the role–playing coppers, sat Bill's
CHRISTIE, 'believable', 'real'.

H.B.

CHRISTIE IN LOVE was first performed by The Portable Theatre at the Ovalhouse, on November 23rd 1969, with the following cast:

CHRISTIE   William Hoyland
CONSTABLE   Matthew Walters
INSPECTOR   Andrew Carr

Directed by David Hare
Stage Management by Snoo Wilson
Set built by Tony Bicât

It was later performed at the Theatre Upstairs, the Royal Court, on March 12th 1970 with the following cast:

CHRISTIE   William Hoyland
CONSTABLE   Brian Croucher
INSPECTOR   Stanley Lebor

Directed by David Hare
Stage Manager Betty Ritchie
Assistant Stage Managers Nick Hart, David Gotthard
Lighting by Gareth Jones

While the audience comes in, the CONSTABLE actor digs in the garden, the INSPECTOR actor stands at the back, the CHRISTIE actor lies concealed beneath the newspaper. A tape broadcasts the facts again and again.

TAPE: John Reginald Halliday Christie was born in Halifax, April of 1898.
He hated his mother, his father and his sisters.
His childhood was normal.
December of 1938, Christie moved with his wife to London.
His marriage was normal.
In March of 1953, Police arrested Christie for murder.
In Christie's London house, the Police found the following corpses.

Buried in the garden, a Miss Eady.
Buried in the garden, a Miss Fuerst.
Hanging in the concealed kitchen alcove, a Miss
MacLennan.
Hanging in the concealed kitchen alcove, a Miss Maloney.
Hanging in the concealed kitchen alcove, a Miss Nelson.
Laid beneath the boards of the living room floor, Mrs
Ethel Christie.
Questioned, an old school mate said of Christie 'He kept
himself to himself.'
Christie wrote 'As I gazed down at the still form of my
first victim, I experienced a strange, peaceful thrill.'
Christie was hanged July of 1953.

(When all the audience is in, the tape fades.)

SCENE ONE

The CONSTABLE digs in the garden. Paper falls from the
spade. He continues, very slowly, until everyone present is
looking at the paper, as it falls from the spade. The CON-
STABLE stops. He stares at the paper. He looks up, and
around at the audience. He recites the first limerick. His
recitation is uncomic, deadly.

CONSTABLE: In the Garden of Eden lay Adam.

(A pause.)

In the Garden of Eden lay Adam
Complacently stroking his madam.
Very loud was his mirth,
For on all of the Earth,
There were only two balls, and he had 'em.

(A pause. The CONSTABLE reflects.)

There were only two balls, and he had 'em.

(The CONSTABLE nods to himself. He digs again. Paper
falls from the spade. He stops digging, and looks up.)

There was a young girl named Heather.

(A pause.)

There was a young girl named Heather
Whose cunt was made out of leather.
She made an odd noise,
For attracting the boys,
By flapping the edges together.

(A pause. The CONSTABLE reflects.)

By flapping the edges together.

(The CONSTABLE nods to himself. He digs again. Paper falls from the spade. He stops digging, and looks up.)

A bawdy young rake from Tashkent.

(A pause.)

A bawdy young rake from Tashkent
Had a cock that was horribly bent.
To get over the trouble,
He pushed it in double,
And instead of his coming he went.

(At once the INSPECTOR shouts from the back. The CONSTABLE jerks to attention.)

INSPECTOR: Constable!

CONSTABLE: Sir!

INSPECTOR: What you doing!

CONSTABLE: Digging Sir!

INSPECTOR: Digging for what Constable!

CONSTABLE: Bones Sir!

INSPECTOR: Right! Bones!

CONSTABLE: Digging for bones Sir!

INSPECTOR: Right again! You keep bones on your mind!

CONSTABLE: I've got bones on my mind Sir!

INSPECTOR: Good man! You keep them there and you won't go far wrong!

(A pause.)

INSPECTOR: Get on with it then!

CONSTABLE: Sir!

(The CONSTABLE digs vigorously. After a while, he wearies, slows down and stops. He looks up.)

CONSTABLE: There was an odd fellow named West.

(A pause.)

There was an odd fellow named West
Whose cock came up to his chest.
He said 'I declare',
'I've got no pubic hair',
So he covered his balls with his vest.

INSPECTOR: Constable!

CONSTABLE: Sir!

INSPECTOR: Kind of bones!

(A pause.)

CONSTABLE: Sir?

INSPECTOR: What kind of bones you looking for? Bones of what animal? Of what genus or species?

CONSTABLE: Women's bones, in't it Sir? The bones of...

(The CONSTABLE searches for the word.)

Ladies?

INSPECTOR: Right. How very right you are. The bones of English Ladies. That's what he's been burying down there, somewhere. Burying English Ladies in his garden! We're going to do him for that!

CONSTABLE: We're going to do him for that Sir!

INSPECTOR: I've heard of some nasty things in my life. But burying English Ladies in your own backyard just about takes the candle. Dig 'em up!

CONSTABLE: Right!

(The CONSTABLE starts digging again, vigorously.)

Right!

INSPECTOR: First sign of a bone, give me the word.

CONSTABLE: Right!

INSPECTOR: The mothers of England depend on you.

(The CONSTABLE digs on. After a while, he wearies, slows down and stops. He looks up.)

CONSTABLE: There was a young man from Coombe.

(A pause.)

There was a young man from Coombe
Who was born six months too soon.
He hadn't the luck,
To be got from a fuck,
But a toss off shoved in with a spoon.

(A pause. The CONSTABLE reflects.)

A toss off. Shoved.

(The CONSTABLE shakes his head, appalled. He wipes his brow. The INSPECTOR comes from the back. Looks the garden over. Looks right and left to see if they are private. Takes out a flask, and offers the CONSTABLE a drink. The CONSTABLE hesitates, wary of rank, but accepts and sits on the side of the garden. The INSPECTOR actor tells the following joke in this way — he works out the pace of a bad joke teller, the abominable and humour-less timing, and then exaggerates the pauses. He stretches it to breaking point.)

INSPECTOR: Know the one about the faith healer?

CONSTABLE: Actually, no Sir.

(The INSPECTOR looks around.)

INSPECTOR: Keep this to yourself.

CONSTABLE: Eh, yes Sir.

INSPECTOR: There was this faith healer you see.

(A pause.)

CONSTABLE: Sir?

INSPECTOR: Wait for it.

CONSTABLE: Yes Sir.

(A pause.)

INSPECTOR: There was this faith healer. The most famous in the land. Anything he touched, he...

(A pause.)

CONSTABLE: I see Sir.

INSPECTOR: Cured. He had what you'd call a wonderful touch.

(A pause.)

CONSTABLE: Cured, Sir.

INSPECTOR: Anyway, this faith healer, he got married. And the first time in bed with his wife he ran his hands all over her, and sealed her up.

(A long pause.)

INSPECTOR: Just a little joke between ourselves.

CONSTABLE: Yes Sir. Very funny Sir.

INSPECTOR: Get on with it.

(The INSPECTOR turns away.)

CONSTABLE: Bleeding hell.

(The CONSTABLE puts the spade in once. He stops dead still, staring down. Simultaneously the INSPECTOR, who was walking away, stops dead still. A pause. The CON-

STABLE speaks quietly.)

Oh my God.

(The INSPECTOR turns. A pause. This passage very loudly.)

CONSTABLE: Bone Sir!

INSPECTOR: Bone!

CONSTABLE: Bone here Sir!

INSPECTOR: Bone there!

CONSTABLE: Got a bone here Sir!

INSPECTOR: What dug up a bone!

CONSTABLE: Bone here!

(A pause. The CONSTABLE speaks quietly.)

More than a bone.

(The INSPECTOR goes to see, climbs into the garden. This passage spoken ordinarily.)

What were she? Tart?

INSPECTOR: Who knows?

CONSTABLE: What he do to her?

(The INSPECTOR shrugs.)

INSPECTOR: What he wanted. No more, no less.

(The CONSTABLE gestures at the grave.)

CONSTABLE: It's beyond me. All that.

INSPECTOR: Takes all kinds. The General Public is a dirty animal.

CONSTABLE: It's beyond me.

INSPECTOR: Don't brood on it Lad. There're many ways of pleasure, most of 'em filth.

CONSTABLE: Still beyond me.

(A pause.)

Look at that fucking great slug.

(At once the INSPECTOR and the CONSTABLE stand back to back. They turn round on the audience in unison with each line, shouting out the limerick. They end facing each other, shaking with rage.)

INSPECTOR AND CONSTABLE: THERE WAS A YOUNG MAN FROM BENGAL
WHO WENT TO A FANCY DRESS BALL.

JUST FOR A STUNT,
HE WENT AS A CUNT,
AND WAS HAD BY A DOG IN THE HALL.

(A pause.)

INSPECTOR: Right. Let's pack up and get out of here.

(The INSPECTOR and the CONSTABLE climb out of the garden, and go to the back. They collect a stretcher and a tarpaulin sheet. They come back, open the stretcher beside the grave. They lay the tarpaulin over the corpse. From here, the lights begin a long fade to the end of the scene.)

CONSTABLE: Sir, what you reckon he did?

INSPECTOR: Did?

CONSTABLE: He whip 'em? Make 'em...Adopt poses? Stick feathers on 'em?

INSPECTOR: Lad, I'll give you a word of warning. I been on these pervy cases before. And the word of warning is, don't brood. You brood, and it'll get you down.

CONSTABLE: It could get you down.

INSPECTOR: It could.

CONSTABLE: It is already.

(The CONSTABLE feels his stomach.)

INSPECTOR: Now copper. Have a bash at controlling yourself.

CONSTABLE: I'll have a bash Sir.

INSPECTOR: Get her up.

(They stand, the CONSTABLE at the front of the stretcher, the INSPECTOR at the back.)

Come on my little darling.

(They step out of the garden. They carry the corpse out to the back during this passage, with a funeral step. The light is nearly gone.)

INSPECTOR: Pleasures of the General Public. You see them all, all the fads. How some like it hot, and some like it cold. How some like it live and some like it dead. And sometimes, why, your own fancy is tickled.

(They stop.)

INSPECTOR: We are human.

CONSTABLE: We are human.

(They go on.)

INSPECTOR: So don't brood. Just clear up the mess.

CONSTABLE: I'll do that Sir.

(In near darkness.)

INSPECTOR: Just clear up the mess.

(It's a blackout.)

SCENE TWO

The lights are snapped up. Very bright. The INSPECTOR and the CONSTABLE are businesslike.

INSPECTOR: Ladies and Gents, John Reginald Christie did six women in.

CONSTABLE: The manner in which they were done was not nice.

INSPECTOR: So if anyone feels sick, go ahead. Throw up. We won't mind.

CONSTABLE: If you want to spew, spew.

INSPECTOR: Right. Let's have a look at him shall we.

(The INSPECTOR nods to the stage management. Blackout.)

SCENE THREE

In the blackout.

INSPECTOR: Out you come Reg.

CONSTABLE: Come on out Reggie.

INSPECTOR: John Reginald Christie!

CONSTABLE: Mr Christie Sir, out you come like a good Sir.

INSPECTOR: Come on Reggie. Let's have a look at you.

(The INSPECTOR and the CONSTABLE switch hand lamps on. They let the beams flick over the garden. The tape begins. The CHRISTIE actor raises his hand out of the paper. A beam catches it, then whisks away. The lamps go out. Then come on and off, at the discretion of the actors. The CHRISTIE actor rises from the paper.

He wears a grotesque mask, a papier mâché head that distorts his features. He undoes his fly, and takes out a length of rubber tubing. He lets down his trousers. He blows into the tube. the effect should be that CHRISTIE's activities are obscured, the beams of the hand lamps do not allow the audience a good look. The taped speech is spoken by the CHRISTIE actor.)

TAPE: Love. Love. Reggie knows his mind 'bout love. And Reggie's never been a one for it. S'all bunk. S'all got up by women. Not that I can't handle them. Women. The bloody female. I'm a dab hand with the ways of love and women, when I want. The Casanova of Halifax. I can give what for. When I want. Much of the time I don't want, that's all. Bah. They give me the pip. Women. With little women's things. Brushes. Tweezers. Sanitary towels. Hairclips. Nasty little instruments to cut you. Coming at you with teeth to give you bites. They're violent, women are. The bitches! Coming up to you, getting violent. Start to paw you about. Get you doing things to them. And they doing things to you. My mother cut my hair. Very, very short. Came at me with scissors, the bitch. Gouging. Cutting off my length. I am a private man and I know my rights. I am, also, a dark horse. Women women women...The streets are full of them. In their nasty skirts. You can hear their skirts, rustle rustle. And their shoes like little metal rats, clip clip upon the pavement. All over. And their beady eyes sweeping the area like birds of prey. And their nails folded ready. They're on the look out! Women out at night for men. Scissors in their handbags to cut you off. Slice you where you're private. Each tit a nail to make you bleed. Each mouth a mousetrap. Cheese nearly in your chops when click! Back's broke. And each cunt a bacon slicer whittling manhood away. A woman's body that's a machine for death.

(Panting breaths, the CHRISTIE actor at climax in the garden. Then he throws himself full length. The hand-lamps go out. Silence. Then the tape continues.)

I am not worried. I know what I like. It is no trouble. It is lovely. It is...

(A pause.)

Cooling.

SCENE FOUR

The lights snap on. CHRISTIE with his trousers down. He takes off the head, and blinks. Then buries it. The INSPECTOR is standing by the garden, looking on.

INSPECTOR: Presentable yet, Reg?

(A pause.)

I don't want to bother you if you're not...

(A pause.)

Presentable.

(CHRISTIE blinks at him. Hurriedly pulls up his trousers, does up the fly.)

CHRISTIE: I'm all right. Thank you very much.

INSPECTOR: Oh! You're all right.

(A pause.)

CHRISTIE: I am.

(A pause.)

INSPECTOR: Let's get on with it then.

(The INSPECTOR quickly goes to the back, and comes forward with a battered card table and a battered wooden chair. He sets them in the garden.)

INSPECTOR: Take a chair.

CHRISTIE: Oh. Right.

(CHRISTIE sits on the chair.)

INSPECTOR: Right!

(A pause.)

Good. There we are then. That's it.

(A pause.)

Then. Good.

(A pause.)

Then.

(A pause.)

Ten Rillington Place.

(A pause.)

Your property?

CHRISTIE: My property.

INSPECTOR: Oh, it's <u>your</u> property.

CHRISTIE: That's my home.

INSPECTOR: But I thought you rented.

(A pause.)

I thought you were a rent-paying tenant. OF the property.

CHRISTIE: The house is my home.

INSPECTOR: Your rented home.

CHRISTIE: I said. The house is my home.

INSPECTOR: But the freehold. That's not yours. Reggie I can't see, I mean I cannot understand, why you are reluctant to admit that you pay rent. I'm speaking frankly now.

CHRISTIE: Oh ay.

INSPECTOR: Are you saying, you fancy yourself as the landlord?

(A pause.)

You fancy you are a property developer?

(The INSPECTOR smiles, chuckles at the absurdity. CHRISTIE attempts an imitative chuckle, but fails. He covers up with a slight cough.)

I mean, that's ridiculous, isn't it? You're not, are you?

CHRISTIE: Oh ay.

INSPECTOR: You're just a grubby rent payer.

CHRISTIE: Oh ay.

(The INSPECTOR holds out three fingers.)

INSPECTOR: Three weeks behind.

(A pause.)

In fact, after you left Ten Rillington Place, and before Constable Thomas picked you up on the embankment at two o'clock in the morning, the landlord came round and found, not only that you owe two weeks, but you had sublet the flat for the sum of seven pounds ten shillings in advance. Sublet illegally. I'm not criticising you Reg. Not for that anyway. But you're no bigtime owner of property.

(A pause.)

CHRISTIE: Oh ay.

INSPECTOR: Still, be that as it may. Tiny isn't it?

(A pause.)

A tiny place.

CHRISTIE: It's a small house.

INSPECTOR: Cramped.

CHRISTIE: It's on the small side.

INSPECTOR: So you'd agree. It's cramped.

CHRISTIE: I said, it's a small house.

(Suddenly the INSPECTOR shouts.)

INSPECTOR: It's fucking cramped!

CHRISTIE: Oh ay. It's...

(A pause.)

Cramped all right.

INSPECTOR: You could say crammed.

CHRISTIE: You could say that.

INSPECTOR: Crammed with, eh, people?

CHRISTIE: There are a lot.

INSPECTOR: Why there's your Mrs, but then she's moved away hasn't she? Gone off? Still it's tiny and there's you downstairs. Poor old Mr Kitchener on the first floor. And on the top there's that young couple, the Evans's.

CHRISTIE: Browns.

INSPECTOR: Oh. Silly of me. Of course. The Browns were involved in that affair weren't they? Timothy Brown. Did his wife and little baby in.

CHRISTIE: No. Evans.

INSPECTOR: What?

CHRISTIE: Timothy Evans. Did his wife and little baby in.

(The INSPECTOR slaps his thigh.)

INSPECTOR: I am a stupid clot! Evans was the bloke not Brown. Course you helped us a lot there, didn't you Reggie. Timothy Evans did his wife and kid in, and stuck 'em in the washhouse out the back of your property. you helped us a lot.

CHRISTIE: I did my bit.

INSPECTOR: You did.

CHRISTIE: I did my bit for public good.

INSPECTOR: And you're going to do your bit again
Reginald. Aren't you?

(A pause.)

CHRISTIE: I'll give what help's within my power.

(The INSPECTOR is delighted.)

INSPECTOR: You mean that?

CHRISTIE: Oh ay.

(The INSPECTOR is suddenly brisk.)

INSPECTOR: Good. First point. The house you rent is
crammed full not only of living, rent-paying tenants
like yourself, but crammed full of dead women.

(A pause.)

I say women loosely. Most of 'em far as the pathologists
can tell were tarts. The real dregs, and hardly a loss
to humanity. But women, tarts, ladies or bleeding
duchesses, your small house is stuffed to the roof
with their remains.

(A pause.)

Now I don't want to get emotional. And I know that you
are not an emotional man. So there is no reason to get
het up. But I got to ask you this Reg. Can you help us
with our enquiries?

(CHRISTIE sits stock still on his chair for a second,
then shifts slightly.)

For example. The 22nd of June last year, a very hot
day, you were observed by a tenant to be sprinkling
Jeyes' Fluid in the passage. Between ourselves, man
to man, couldn't you stand the smell?

(At once, CHRISTIE half rises from his chair.)

CHRISTIE: I'm not going to sit here...

INSPECTOR: Oh you are. You are going to sit there.

(CHRISTIE sits. The INSPECTOR smiles.)

INSPECTOR: Remember, you are not an emotional man.

CHRISTIE: No. I don't like to let my feelings show.

INSPECTOR: Stiff upper lip!

(The INSPECTOR laughs.)

Everyone in the street says that of you, all your neigh-
bours. Mr Christie keeps a stiff upper lip. Keeps himself to himself. Keeps...Neat.

(A pause.)

All right we'll forget about the Jeyes for the time being.
Why shouldn't a householder that is a rent-paying tenant
keep his place sanitary? Jeyes is just the thing in hot
weather. Clean and pungent, overriding any other odour.
I'm not unreasonable Reg. I'm not going off on an
emotional tack. Like accusing you of doing your Mrs in
and burying her under the floorboards in the front room.
From where, by the way, we dug her up the other day.
I mean I'm not going off at a tangent. I just don't know
where to begin. But I wondered if you could help.

(A pause.)

With a few details.

(A pause.)

Like why you killed those tarts.

(A pause.)

And did you fuck them before or after?

(Blackout.)

SCENE FIVE

Lit by a camera flashbulb, CHRISTIE rises, leans over the
table and masturbates. On the tape women's voices call out,
overlapping and laughing.

TAPE:...Reggie.
...Reggie Weggie.
...Reggie No Dick.
...Where is you Reggie?
...What you doing Reggie?
...It dirty Reggie?
...It nasty?
...Nasty little boy we going to get you.
...Reginald! Stop that at once!
...Going to get Reggie No Dick.
...Reggie! Stop that nasty thing!
...Going to cut off Reggie Weggie's Dicky Wick.

(The lights are snapped up. CHRISTIE whirls round,
looking at the audience section by section, terrified. He
sits down. By a series of gestures, he attempts to re-
cover – he hitches his trousers, straightens his tie,
smoothes his lapels.)

SCENE SIX

The INSPECTOR approaches CHRISTIE, holding out a glass phial.

INSPECTOR: Know what this is? It intimately concerns you.

CHRISTIE: Oh ay.

INSPECTOR: It is your semen Reginald.

> (A pause.)

> The Christie family jewels. Hot stuff, eh Reg? You reckon that's hot stuff?

> (The INSPECTOR steps into the garden, and shoves the phial under CHRISTIE's nose.)

> Eh? Go on have a whiff. Don't mind me.

> (CHRISTIE leans back, to avoid the phial. The IN-SPECTOR puts the phial on the table.)

> Medical Science tells us there are millions of potential little Reginalds in that tube.

> (The INSPECTOR shakes his head.)

> What a waste. But you did not encourage them to come to fruition did you. The use you put your spunk to did not encourage birth.

> (CHRISTIE mumbles, indistinctly.)

CHRISTIE: You're being bloody personal.

INSPECTOR: What you say Reg? Speak up.

CHRISTIE: You're being bloody personal.

INSPECTOR: Enunciate with clarity you fucking pervert.

CHRISTIE: Bloody personal!

> (CHRISTIE puts his hand to his chest.)

> Gas. Got load in First War.

INSPECTOR: What? What?

CHRISTIE: Got load of gas. 1918. Three years, couldn't speak.

INSPECTOR: Ah! Your war disability.

CHRISTIE: Honourably disabled.

> (CHRISTIE breathes heavily.)

INSPECTOR: You sniveller. I dunno, it's disappointing. Why can't a mass murderer be just a bit diabolical? Why can't a pervert like you, already in the annals of nastiness, have fangs or something? Roll your eyes around. Sprout horns.

(The INSPECTOR kicks up the paper in a fury.)

Go on Reg, let's have a real bit of horror!

(A pause. CHRISTIE speaks weakly.)

CHRISTIE: I've overlooked my inhaler. Could you send round for it? Do you think? For my catarrh?

(The INSPECTOR shakes his head, saddened.)

INSPECTOR: And Madame Tussauds has been onto us all day for a plaster cast of your head.

CHRISTIE: My inhaler.

INSPECTOR: No you can't have your bloody inhaler!

CHRISTIE: I got my rights.

INSPECTOR: That inhaler is the property of the Crown. We don't know what you been up to with it, do we.

CHRISTIE: I don't know what you're inferring.

INSPECTOR: Lots Reg. The whole filthy bundle I'm inferring.

CHRISTIE: If I don't have my inhaler, I'll come over with an attack.

(The INSPECTOR speaks confidentially.)

INSPECTOR: Don't threaten me.

(A pause. The INSPECTOR points at the phial.)

Forensics, Reg. It is all a matter of traces. The chalky soil from the flowerbed on the cat thief's boot. The telltale powder burn on the bank robber's sleeve. To the forensic scientist the criminal is always leaving his signature. It may be his finger prints. His dandruff. His spit, or his urine. Or, as in your case, his sperm.

(A pause.)

The dead tarts, Reg. They're full of your stuff. Science knows you fucked them all.

SCENE SEVEN

CHRISTIE and the INSPECTOR freeze. The CONSTABLE
has been drinking at the back.

CONSTABLE: Bloody hell!

(The CONSTABLE stumbles to the centre.)

Oh bloody hell. I'm bloody overwhelmed. Went home to
my Mrs. You smell she said. Course I smelled, all day
digging in his graveyard. Had three baths in a row.
Disinfected me all over. Scrubbed me nails. Pumiced me
palms. No good! Me Mrs could smell 'em. The dead
women on me. I could not stand the look my very own
and loved and cherished gave me. Went round the pub.
Started to knock it back. And it all went round in my
head. Him. In his kitchen he had a tin, Old Holborn
'baccy tin, of two ounce size. Know what he had in that
tin? Pubic hairs, cut off the women he had. Bloody hell.
He cut off their pubic hairs and kept them in a tin. I tell
you its all too...

(The CONSTABLE searches for the word.)

Deep, for me.

(The CONSTABLE stumbles to the back, and kneels
down by the DOLL on the stretcher.)

SCENE EIGHT

INSPECTOR: Our pathologists conclude, the women were
getting cold. You had'em dead, didn't you.

(CHRISTIE stands violently, and knocks over the table
and chair.)

INSPECTOR: Finally got to your bent have we? Touch of
the necrophiliacs, eh?

(At the same time the CONSTABLE picks up the DOLL
in his arms, and talks to her.)

CONSTABLE: Eh my love? What? What? I dunno.

INSPECTOR: Like your women drained of blood? Like
your women cooled off? Don't work any other way for
you, eh? Got to get 'em ready, hang 'em up stuck
like a pig? If you weren't a well known anti-semite
I'd say you were after a good kosher fuck.

(CHRISTIE faints, full length. He crawls feebly in the

paper. The lights begin to fade.)

Tell me how you really like it. Love. I will not be shocked. I am a policeman of the realm. I am conversant with it all. The sinks and sewers of the minds of men and women. I spend my professional life in the General Public's shithouse. I am a father to your kind, Reg. Tell your father.

(The light is almost gone.)

SCENE NINE

Red light. The INSPECTOR goes to the back. The CONSTABLE comes forward with the DOLL in his arms circles the garden, showing her to the audience.

CONSTABLE: Just a scrubber. Twenty-six. Tits a bit worn. The rest of her, a bit worn. A very ordinary bint. I wouldn't have minded a go. I mean, if she weren't a rotting corpse I'd have, perhaps, chanced my arm.

(CHRISTIE stands.)

CHRISTIE: NO ONE PLAYS THE FOOL WI' ME. SEE? NO MAN NO WOMAN. PLAYS THE FOOL WI' ME.

(CHRISTIE lifts a foot.)

See my plims?

(CHRISTIE steps out of the garden.)

No woman ever knows if I'm near or not. I pass like a ghost through Society. The petty criminal in his den, the tart in her red room. I come and go, a military looking gent. A good citizen, in plims.

CONSTABLE: She were only a common day fuck. That's all. Used, yeh, but a common...

(He searches for the word.)

Woman.

(To CHRISTIE.)

So what you have to go and do perversions for? She offer first? Or did you have to force your foul desire? And what she say when she first approached? She say...

(The CONSTABLE actor holds the DOLL before him, and works the arms and head for occasional gestures. He speaks the woman's part, in a falsetto voice, over the DOLL's shoulder.)

DOLL: Want a touch love?

(A pause.)

Want a touch love?

(A pause.)

Want a touch love?

CHRISTIE: No one touches me!

DOLL: Sorry I'm sure.

(She turns away.)

CHRISTIE: Eh up there.

(She turns back.)

DOLL: What?

CHRISTIE: Want to touch me do you?

DOLL: All the same to me love. Touch or not touch, if the price is right.

CHRISTIE: Bloody tarts! Coming up, touching you!

DOLL: All right, all right.

CHRISTIE: Want to get your hands on me don't you. Get your fingers. On. Want to poke me.

DOLL: I don't have to stand here and talk to you. There're too many queer fishes about nowadays. A girl's not safe. The Government should do something.

(She turns away.)

CHRISTIE: Eh up there.

(She stops, and turns back.)

DOLL: Do you don't you? Make up your bleeding mind.

CHRISTIE: See my plims?

DOLL: Very nice.

CHRISTIE: I creep about in them.

DOLL: I don't doubt it.

CHRISTIE: I come up unawares in them.

DOLL: Do you.

CHRISTIE: Then I pounce.

DOLL: That's not very nice, is it.

CHRISTIE: It ain't nice come to think of it. Come to think of it, it's...Nasty.

DOLL: It's very nasty.

CHRISTIE: Women bring out the nastiness in me.

DOLL: Do they.

CHRISTIE: They bring it out. And they love it, the stupid bitches. That's all they want. To be kicked about a bit. Be scared to shits. You scared to shits, girly?

DOLL: Cost you money to scare me.

CHRISTIE: How much?

DOLL: Two quid.

CHRISTIE: One pound ten.

DOLL: Thirty-five bob.

CHRISTIE: Thirty-five bob.

DOLL: I'm scared.

CHRISTIE: Ha!

(CHRISTIE backs away, pointing at her.)

Ha!

(He holds out his police identification. She peers at it.)

DOLL: Constable John Reginald Christie. You're a fucking dick.

CHRISTIE: Just a Special.

DOLL: Still a fucking dick.

CHRISTIE: Still very much a fucking dick.

DOLL: What a come on. You deliberately encouraged my soliciting, pretending you were a queer fish just to get a girl arrested.

CHRISTIE: I'm a respectable citizen girly. I was gassed in the First World War. Couldn't speak for three year. I served my country.

DOLL: An amateur policeman. Just my luck.

CHRISTIE: Watch your lip yer whore.

(A pause.)

DOLL: Well come on. Take my name. Take my address. Take me down the station for a good laugh with your friends.

(A pause.)

What you waiting for?

(A pause.)

Ruth Fuerst, 27, Ladbroke Grove. Twenty-six years old. I'm not wholly on the game. I would describe myself as an experienced amateur. I have prostitutes among my friends. I work as a nurse. I get bored a lot.

CHRISTIE: Do it for free.

(A pause.)

You don't want to be charged for soliciting.

DOLL: You making a proposition?

CHRISTIE: Little arrangement.

DOLL: Stone me. If I take my knickers down to you, you let me go?

CHRISTIE: Don't be coarse.

DOLL: I'll believe anything of the police force now.

CHRISTIE: You keep respectful.

DOLL: I do it, you let me go. I don't do it, I get charged for prostitution. That really takes the pip.

(A pause.)

Haven't got much choice, have I?

CHRISTIE: None.

DOLL: I think that I'm in your power.

(The CHRISTIE actor embraces the DOLL. He takes her arm, they walk round two sides of the garden. CHRISTIE steps into the garden, the CONSTABLE actor follows, with the DOLL. CHRISTIE goes to a corner and fiddles with a cup and saucer and a teapot.)

DOLL: What a filthy house.

CHRISTIE: It's clean enough.

DOLL: What's all this stuff?

CHRISTIE: It's clean I said! Spotless.

DOLL: All right.

CHRISTIE: There's no dirt here!

DOLL: All right, all right!

(She speaks aside.)

He is a queer fish. THOUGH I've had queer fish in my time, AND left 'em to swim away. If you get my meaning. Here we go.

(The CONSTABLE actor strips off the Doll's clothes.)

'Ere. What you doing out there?

CHRISTIE: Making cup of tea.

DOLL: Highly romantic. Two lumps please.

(CHRISTIE, to himself.)

CHRISTIE: Two lumps eh? Two lumps eh?

DOLL: Could do with a cup of tea.

(CHRISTIE, cup and saucer in one hand teapot in the other, whirls on her.)

CHRISTIE: Who said you were getting a cup?

DOLL: Ooh la la. Sorry I spoke I'm sure.

CHRISTIE: Tea's for after. That's how I like it, after.

DOLL: Come on then. Let's get it over with.

SCENE TEN

The INSPECTOR comes forward. CHRISTIE puts his hands on the DOLL. He speaks to the INSPECTOR.

CHRISTIE: I have something on my mind. It comes back to me in flashes. If it does come back, I will tell you, I truly will.

(CHRISTIE puts his hand between the DOLL's legs.)

CONSTABLE: Hello! I think he's off.

CHRISTIE: I don't remember what happened. But I must have gone haywire.

(The INSPECTOR hands CHRISTIE a short length of rope. CHRISTIE whips it round the DOLL's neck, and strangles her.)

CONSTABLE: Sir! He's off! He's well away!

(And CHRISTIE has gone down, still pulling the rope tight. The CONSTABLE ends up in the paper, under the DOLL, CHRISTIE on top of them both. CHRISTIE lets go the rope.)

CHRISTIE: The next thing I remember she was lying down, a rope about her neck. I left her there and went into the front room. I had a cup of tea, and I went to bed. I got up in the morning, and washed and shaved. She still lay there. I had a cup of tea. I pulled away a cup—

board and gained access to a small alcove. I knew it
was there because a pipe burst in the frosty weather
and a plumber opened it up to mend the pipe.

CONSTABLE: This is getting out of hand. Right out.

CHRISTIE: I was in love with her.

SCENE ELEVEN

The lights change from red to bright white. The CONSTABLE
throws the DOLL and CHRISTIE off of him, and rises to
make his protest.

CONSTABLE: That's not love.

INSPECTOR: Is to him.

CONSTABLE: Dead bodies?

(CHRISTIE takes up the DOLL, and carries her on his
knees to the other side of the garden, and buries her
as best he can in the newspaper.)

CHRISTIE: Took her out the back. Wrapped her up in old
newspaper. Buried her.

CONSTABLE: Love's the bleeding moon. And bleeding doves
cooing. And bleeding Frank Sinatra crooning. And
holding hands. And a lovely bunch of roses from the one
whom you admire. And a nice church ceremony, and the
Mrs tearful eyed at the photograph. We went to Clacton
for our honeymoon, my wife and me. The sea was
gentle as a baby. The moon was smoochy yellow. That
were love. Not a corpse, in a dirty garden.

(During his speech, the INSPECTOR sets the chair in
the centre of the garden, stands on it, and rigs a
noose up through the rafters.)

INSPECTOR: One bloke we nicked, had a thing about handbags. Couldn't keep himself out of them. 'Nother bloke
we nicked, had a thing about pussycats. The handbag
man we got for shop lifting. The pussycat man we got
for cruelty to animals. See Reg, you got to keep love
in bounds. Else it gets criminal. And we can't have
that, can we.

(Standing on the chair. the INSPECTOR bellows to all
the audience.)

Society cannot allow the fucking of handbags. Pussycats.
Dead women. What would happen if we all went right
ahead, according to desire, fucking all? Bleeding

anarchy Reg. Larceny, mutilation of animals, murder.

(The police shout angrily at CHRISTIE, who is still kneeling over the DOLL's grave.)

CONSTABLE: You filthy beast! You utter cad!

INSPECTOR: Bloody pervert!

CONSTABLE: Bloody pervert!

INSPECTOR: Go one better than us would you, eh? Eh? Defile English Womanhood?

CONSTABLE: Cast aspersions on my mother!

INSPECTOR: Cast aspersions would you!

(The CONSTABLE, all self control gone, grabs CHRISTIE, who's limp and barely whispers, and drags him up to the noose. The Police hang CHRISTIE. CHRISTIE falls into the paper, the noose still about his neck. A pause. The INSPECTOR steps down from the chair, straightens his uniform. Both policemen are shaken, shamefaced.)

INSPECTOR: That's that then.

CONSTABLE: Yes Sir.

INSPECTOR: Another crime solved.

CONSTABLE: A blow struck for married life.

INSPECTOR: Yes.

CONSTABLE: Yes.

(The INSPECTOR puts the chair upside down on the table, picks the table up, about to carry it off. He stops.)

INSPECTOR: Just...Clean up a bit. Someone else's garden now.

CONSTABLE: Sir.

INSPECTOR: Get on with it then.

CONSTABLE: Sir.

(The CONSTABLE covers the body of CHRISTIE with the spade, slowly, smoothes the surface of the paper down, then looks around the audience, shamefaced, and slips away. End play.)

Heads

HEADS was first presented by the University of Bradford
Drama Group in June 1969 with the following cast:

MEGAN   Michele Ryan
ROCK   Phillip Emmanuel
BRIAN   Greg Philo

Directed by Chris Parr
Stage Manager Jo Stell

It was subsequently presented by Inter-Action at the
Ambiance-In-Exile Lunch Hour Theatre Club on March 2nd
1970 with the following cast:

MEGAN   Frances Tomelty
ROCK   Christopher Martin
BRIAN   Michael Feast

Directed by Roland Rees
Stage Manager Roy Preston
Lighting by Nick Garnet

MICHELE, GREG and PHIL in a circle. PHIL begins to
limber up. GREG is reading a book. MICHELE stands
aside, sexily.

PHIL: Rock is my name and that sums up my body. Rock
    hard. Hup!

    (PHIL exercises.)

    Women have remarked before on my body. One woman
    said to me, Rock you're a symphony of gristle. Said
    she heard music everytime I flexed myself. Hup!

    (PHIL exercises.)

GREG: I've always been rather...

    (GREG twitches.)

    Bright. When I was five, I performed the world's first
    heart transplant. On my Noddy. I got the heart from
    Big Ears. Of course it wasn't really a heart, just...

(GREG twitches.)

Stuffing.

MICHELE: Those are my two men, and I love them both for their various attributes. There a beautiful body, there a beautiful brain.

PHIL: I can't read much. Can't read at all, actually. Not that I got anything against books. I first showed my strength on a book. I was five years old at Sunday School and I tore up the Holy Bible, just like that. Hup!

(PHIL exercises, then stops, and speaks reverently.)

Course I did not know it was God's Word. Or any other Word. A word to me is just a blur. The Holy Bible, The North Eastern Railway Time Table, The Thoughts Of Chairman Mao Tse Tung. All a blur, to me.

(Sadly.)

Sometimes I wish I could read the little bastards, read the little blurs. La-dies, Gent-le-men.

(Fiercely.)

But I don't care. I don't need to read. I got my body and I'm happy. Hup!

(PHIL exercises.)

GREG: At school they called me boffin. They also called me The Mekon. They also called me Weed. And...

(GREG twitches.)

Twiggy. I was not popular. In gym periods when I took off my shirt they all cried Boneyard! Then I was exempted from gym and games, because of my asthma.

(Bitterly.)

Muscles are for cattle, who end as meat. It's not true all girls admire is muscular development. You don't need to twiddle your biceps when you've got a lively mind for girls to love.

(MICHELE goes up to PHIL.)

MICHELE: Hello Rock.

PHIL: Hello Fruitcake.

MICHELE: How are you Rock.

PHIL: Bulging my love. Have a feel.

(PHIL offers his biceps. MICHELE is shocked.)

MICHELE: Rock!

PHIL: Go on. You know you love that rippling sensation.

MICHELE: That's all you think of. Body body.

> (A pause. PHIL flexes his biceps a few times, then speaks excitedly.)

PHIL: Crumpet.

MICHELE: What.

PHIL: They've come!

MICHELE: What have come?

PHIL: In the post this morning.

MICHELE: What, for crying out loud?

PHIL: My Mr Universe Big B Briefs.

MICHELE: Your what?

PHIL: My Mr Universe Big B Briefs.

MICHELE: Oh Rock, you've not replied to an advert on the back of the Radio Times, again.

PHIL: I've got them on underneath. Want a butchers?

MICHELE: No I do not want a butchers.

PHIL: What's the matter Crumpet? They show me off a treat.

MICHELE: I don't doubt it.

PHIL: They're as worn by Mr Universe himself. Make a great deal of sense out of my stance. Bags of lift.

MICHELE: Oh Rock, I wish you'd give up Physical Culture.

PHIL: Give up Physical Culture? You don't know what you're saying. I'd go flabby. Don't want me flabby do you? Not with a name like Rock.

MICHELE: I don't care.

PHIL: You don't care if I run to fat?

MICHELE: I don't. It's you I love, not your body.

PHIL: But I am my body.

MICHELE: You're Rock.

PHIL: That's right. Rock's body.

MICHELE: Body body body. What about your head?

PHIL: My head? I got good neck muscles. Bulge a treat when I grit my teeth.

> (PHIL grits his teeth.)

Have a feel.

MICHELE: I don't want to feel your muscles anymore.
It's disgusting. You're always asking me to feel your
muscles.

(PHIL is crestfallen.)

PHIL: You used to say they made you tingle.

MICHELE: What about your mind?

(A pause.)

PHIL: My what?

MICHELE: Your mind. Your thoughts.

PHIL: Yeh. Well.

(PHIL's lost.)

What?

MICHELE: What about poetry?

PHIL: Yeh.

(PHIL frowns.)

MICHELE: Intellectual pursuits. The discussion of inter-
national affairs. Bartok's String Quartets.

PHIL: You getting at me?

MICHELE: Your thoughts Rock. What do you think?

PHIL: What do I think?

MICHELE: What do you think?

PHIL: I think...How good it is. Yeh. When I've had a stiff
work out, and have a shower, I think how good that is.
Yeh.

(A pause.)

You are getting at me. Don't get at me, Fruitcake. I
don't like being got at. I lose control. I don't want to
lose control with you, you're nice. So don't get at me.

MICHELE: You great thick ha'p'orth. I'm sick of the smell
of body oil. Sick of flesh flesh flesh.

PHIL: I'm sorry.

(MICHELE backs away.)

MICHELE: It's not all body, you know.

PHIL: Not all body? What else is there then? Other? What
else, other than body?

(PHIL looks at his hands.)

Bone and gristle, that's you. Eight pints of blood.
Millions of little nerves, hundres of muscles in constant
play. That's your body and that's you. All the rest is...

(PHIL makes a gesture of disgust.)

Talk.

(MICHELE goes up to GREG.)

MICHELE: Hello Brian.

GREG: Oh. Hello there.

MICHELE: How are you Brian.

GREG: Brushing up my vocabulary. Ask me a word.

MICHELE: Um. Palindrome?

GREG: Noun. Word, line, etc., that reads back and forwards
e.g. MADAM. Greek, meaning palin, again, psao, rub,
dromos, run.

MICHELE: Um. Osmosis?

GREG: Neuter noun. Tendency of fluids, separated by
membrance or other porous substance, to percolate and
mix.

MICHELE: Give me a kiss.

(MICHELE closes her eys. GREG is embarassed.)

GREG: Noun. Caress with lips. In billiards impact between
moving balls. Verb transitive. Touch with the lips.

(GREG goes to kiss her, but retreats, and continues
desperately.)

Kiss hands, sovereign's hand on appointment as
minister. Kiss the dust, yield, abject submission, drop
dead. Kiss the rod, accept submission submissively.
Kiss-in-the-ring, a game. Kissing-crust, soft crust
where loaf has touched another in baking. Kissing-
gate, hung in U or V shaped enclosure. Don't do that!

MICHELE: Do what?

GREG: Pucker up your mouth.

MICHELE: Sometimes Brian, I wonder if you're frigid.

(GREG with self-loathing.)

GREG: Adverb. Cold. Lacking ardour. Formal. Forced.
Dull.

MICHELE: Sometimes I look at you reading poetry with

your legs crossed and think 'he's not natural'.

GREG: Not natural?

MICHELE: Unhealthy.

GREG: Ah!

MICHELE: What do you mean Ah!

GREG: Big cocks.

MICHELE: Brian!

GREG: I thought you loved a lively mind. But it's big cocks in the end. That's what it comes down to, in the end. Length.

MICHELE: You've got a morbid mind, that's what.

GREG: If you met Socrates you'd not ask him the secret of of the Universe. You'd ask him how big a cock he had.

MICHELE: And who was Socrates?

GREG: A fat old man.

MICHELE: I hate fat old men.

GREG: He was a monumental intellect!

MICHELE: I don't care. He was a fat old man and no doubt dirty too.

GREG: Actually he was homosexual.

MICHELE: There you are. That's where thinking gets you. Going against nature.

(MICHELE stamps her foot, and turns away. A pause, then GREG, shyly.)

GREG: How about a Violin Sonata.

(A pause.)

A Harpsichord Concerto.

MICHELE: Go away, you're queer.

(MICHELE turns her back on both of them. PHIl goes up to GREG.)

PHIL: Tough, eh mate?

GREG: What?

PHIL: Tough, when you've got bags of what they don't want.

GREG: Yes.

PHIL: I wish the brain didn't count.

GREG: I wish the body didn't count.

PHIL: I wish I were all animal.

GREG: I wish I were all intellect.

PHIL: I'd be free.

GREG: I'd be free.

PHIL: I'd be a horse. An Arabian steed of shiny flank, galloping over the desert. No thoughts just run run run in a world of sky and sand.

GREG: I'd be a brain. Only a brain. Suspended in jelly in a metal box. I'd have a loudspeaker on top of the box, to broadcast my thoughts. I'd be quite still, and just think.

PHIL: You wouldn't get around at all?

GREG: Maybe I'd have little wheels.

(MICHELE aside.)

MICHELE: All a girl wants is a husband, that's all. A good male body, strong enough, no TB, sexy enough. Brains up to a point, to work out the mortgage and the hire purchase. Don't want a Samson pulling buildings apart, don't want an Einstein living in the fourth dimension.

PHIL: If you were a brain, trundling round on wheels, what about women?

GREG: What about them?

PHIL: Be a bit difficult wouldn't it?

GREG: I don't see why.

PHIL: Difficult, having it off.

GREG: I see what you mean.

(A pause.)

We wouldn't.

PHIL: Oh.

MICHELE: Megan, my Ma said, Megan, beware of extremes and the men who go to them. Extremes bring Bailiff and Constable to the door.

PHIL: You'd not have it off at all?

GREG: Not exactly.

PHIL: No.

(PHIL frowns.)

Not exactly.

GREG: It would be a meeting of minds. We'd park next to
each other and...Exchange information. Sort of
caress each other's nerve ends.

(PHIL shakes his head.)

PHIL: Be a horse mate.

MICHELE: Megan, my Ma said, Megan, a man is a soggy
bit of putty. You mould him to what you will. The
woman makes the man, Megan. But Ma, I said, they
told us in Sunday School the woman came from the rib.
That's all propaganda she said, trumped up by males.
Genesis was written by a man. Remember Megan, in
the Old Religion God was a woman.

(A pause. Then MICHELE, with formality.)

These are my two men, and I love them both for their
various attributes. What a pity what a joke, that they
are made so extremely. What a pity what a joke, that
that brain and that body
are not moulded in one
wholly normal normally whole
and lovely
man.

(MICHELE points slowly from PHIL's head to GREG's,
from GREG's head to PHIL's, and thinks. Then snaps
her fingers.)

MICHELE: What I need's an axe, and glue.

(Blackout. A tape, 'Here comes a chopper to chop off
your head...', chopping sounds, and screams. The
screams continue for one minute. Lights up. Silence.
GREG and PHIL have changed clothes, and are back
to back in the centre of the circle. PHIL is Rock's
head on Brian's body. MICHELE stands aside, her
arms are covered with tomato ketchup, in one hand she
holds an axe, in the other a big tube of glue.

Note. Dear GREG and PHIL. Don't set yourself too
much with this scene. Just follow the routine. Don't
scream indiscriminately, 'Wha' means 'What?' Its a
dialogue, question and answer between the two
mutilations.)

GREG: Wha?

(PHIL starts at the sound, and jerks his head to one side.)

Wha?

PHIL: Wha?

(A pause. They both stagger forward a few steps. The calls to each other get loud, then very loud.)

GREG: Wha?

PHIL: Wha?

(A pause.)

GREG: Wha!

PHIL: Wha?

GREG: WHA?

(A pause.)

GREG: WHA?

PHIL: WHA?

GREG: WHA?

PHIL: WHA?

GREG: WHA?

PHIL: WHA?

GREG: WHA?

PHIL: WHA?

GREG: WHA?

(A pause. A count of three. PHIL and GREG whirl round and stare at each other. A pause. Jerkily, they look down each other's body, to the feet. A pause. They jerk their heads up again, and stare. A pause. They each turn their attention to themselves. Then PHIL, as the weak head now on the weak body, crouches down with a little whimper. GREG, as the strong head now on the strong body, is catching on.)

MICHELE: Brian's head on Rock's body, oh you lovely creature.

GREG: Marry me.

MICHELE: Of course, silly.

(GREG stumbles forward and embraces her. At the same time, PHIL comes forward on his hands and knees to the centre. From now to the end, MICHELE is impassive, standing with the instruments.)

PHIL: Went off. Right away. Weak head on weakling body. Poor me, poor leftovers. Went away, right away, live now in a cave, eat berries, talk to no one. Mornings wake up, think go for a run. Fifty press ups, bit of weight lifting. But then look down, see my weedy body, pain in the chest, acne under armpits, biceps like a baby's, balls like little marbles two a penny. So I stay in my cave all day, eat berries, talk to no one.

(GREG breaks away from MICHELE, and comes to the 'mouth of the cave'.)

GREG: Rock!

PHIL: In here.

(GREG 'crawls into the cave.')

GREG: Hello Rock.

PHIL: Hello, Brian.

GREG: I've left her, Rock.

PHIL: Oh yeh.

GREG: She's a monster. I lived in constant fear of further mutilations.

PHIL: You'd think she'd done enough.

(A pause.)

How's the body?

GREG: I can't stand it, Rock.

PHIL: Why not? That's a good body. You've not let it get run down? I'll not forgive you, if you've let it get run down.

GREG: It's very fit.

PHIL: I should hope so. I spent a lot of time on it.

GREG: It has its own momentum.

(A pause.)

How's the rash, under the arms?

PHIL: Know about that, do you?

GREG: Had it since I was a child.

PHIL: It's bad.

GREG: Don't scratch, that makes it worse. I thought it would be bad, I brought some Valderma.

(GREG gives PHIL a tube of Valderma.)

PHIL: Thanks.

GREG: Not going to put it on?

PHIL: I've not got the interest really.

GREG: No.

PHIL: No.

   (A pause.)

   What we going to do, Brian?

GREG: Could have an operation.

PHIL: Could have, I s'pose.

   (A pause.)

GREG: Could burn ourselves with petrol.

PHIL: We could.

GREG: Self-immolation.

PHIL: Yeh. I s'pose.

   (A pause.)

GREG: Seems a pity, though.

PHIL: Let's live here. In my cave. We got to face it, we're freaks. We'll live here.

GREG: What about food?

PHIL: Berries do all right for your body.

GREG: Yours cries out for meat.

PHIL: We'll knock off the occasional sheep. We may be freaks, but life can go on. Can't it? Can, can't it?

GREG: Let me see that rash.

PHIL: Let me see how the old biceps are doing.

   (GREG raises PHIL's arm, then squeezes some Valderma and applies it to PHIL's armpit. PHIl takes GREG's free arm by the wrist, and works it up and down. Both are absorbed. MICHELE standing with the bloody axe. The lights go down slowly. End play.)

The Education of Skinny Spew

THE EDUCATION OF SKINNY SPEW was first presented by the University of Bradford Drama Group in June 1969 with the following cast:

SKINNY SPEW   Greg Philo
MRS SPEW, etc. Michele Ryan
MR SPEW, etc.   Phillip Emmanuel

Directed by Chris Parr
Stage Manager Jo Stell

It was subsequently presented by Inter-Action at the Ambiance-In-Exile Lunch Hour Theatre Club on March 2nd 1970 with the following cast:

SKINNY SPEW   Michael Feast
MRS SPEW, etc   Frances Tomelty
MR SPEW, etc   Christopher Martin

Directed by Roland Rees
Stage Manager Roy Preston
Lighting by Nick Garnet

A double white sheet is laid out in the middle of a circle. When the audience are all in, the lights go down. At once a tape of a heartbeat starts. Then GREG speaks as Skinny Spew in the womb, live over a mike. Stage management make the noises of labour, written here as 'Huh', building the rhythm.

SCENE ONE: SKINNY'S BIRTH

GREG: I think, I think I'm in some OLD BAG.

ALL: Huh.

GREG: What kind of old bag? Handbag? Paper bag?

ALL: Huh.

GREG: Whatever kind of bag, its slimy.

ALL: Huh huh.

GREG: Mother bag! A mother bag, that's what I'm in!

Stuffed in my mother's womb!

(A loud BOM on a drum. At once the lights go up.
MICHELE, as Mrs Spew, is lying under the sheet.)

MICHELE: Ow! Doctor doctor!

(PHIL comes forward as the Doctor.)

Doctor doctor, he kicked and awful hard.

PHIL: Little Bobby Charlton is he? Ha ha.

MICHELE: Is he on his way?

PHIL: He's on his way. Out the dressing room, up the
players' tunnel, onto the football pitch of life, ha ha.

GREG: The doctor sounds a right twit.

ALL: Huh huh.

GREG: I think, I think I'll give him a rough time. I think,
I think I'll come out upside down. Or backwards.

ALL: Huh huh.

GREG: I know. I'll startle medical science and come out
through her bum.

ALL: HUH HUH.

(MICHELE writhes. She grabs the top of the sheet
about her throat, in a knot, and holds on tight. PHIL
grabs the other end, and it's a tug of war, with the
sheet between MICHELE's legs.)

MICHELE: Doctor doctor, what's gone wrong?

PHIL: The little bugger.

MICHELE: Ow! He's wriggling about!

(The heart beats get louder. PHIL gets desperate.)

PHIL: Don't worry I'm fully qualified. Nurse! Forceps!

GREG: He thinks I'm a cork in a bottle.

ALL: HUH HUH.

PHIL: One two!

(PHIL tugs.)

MICHELE: Ow!

GREG: Ow!

PHIL: At times like this I wonder why I ever took up surgery. Come on you little runt! One two!

(PHIL tugs.)

MICHELE: Ow!

GREG: Ow!

PHIL: They think a doctor's life is all beauty. One hand on the pulse of nature, the other up a nurse's skirt. One two!

(PHIL tugs.)

MICHELE: Ow!

GREG: Ow!

PHIL: Lance a boil. Chop out some old geezer's gallstones. Drag a baby into the world bloody and puking. It's all butchery. Slash slash slash. Come on you horrible bundle of joy, come on, come on.

(The lights are fading. PHIL is at full stretch tugging the sheet, MICHELE is screaming, the heart beat is very loud.)

ALL: HUH HUH HUH, HUH HUH HUH, HUH HUH HUH HUH.

(Blackout. A short silence. The drum goes BOM. Then GREG is heard on a tape, bawling his head off like a baby.)

SCENE TWO: CHILDHOOD

Lights up. GREG is in the centre, in a pram. He has a teddy bear. PHIL as Mr Spew and MICHELE as Mrs Spew stand by the pram. A pause. It's a family photograph, the mother adoring, the father disgruntled, the baby scowling.

GREG: I just got born. And that's my Mummy. And that's my Daddy. And I think, I think I'll shit my nappies up.

MICHELE: There you are Henry. Our very own little one.

PHIL: I think he's shitting his nappies up.

MICHELE: He's not. He's Mummy's little boy. And Mummy's little boy would not shitty whitty his nappy wappies.

(GREG looks around.)

GREG: She talking to me?

MICHELE: Ogy ogy goo.

GREG: She IS talking to me.

MICHELE: A little one, after all these years! Woogy woogy wiggy wiggy.

GREG: I know I'm a baby. But she's carrying on like I was a moron. I think I'll give her what for.

(GREG throws the teddy bear out of the pram.)

Waa. Waa.

(MICHELE picks up the teddy bear, and gives it back to GREG. GREG snatches it, and glares at her.)

PHIL: He looks a bit pasty.

MICHELE: They always look like that.

PHIL: He's got scabs on his mouth.

MICHELE: That's quite normal.

PHIL: There's snot running out of his nose.

MICHELE: That's normal too.

PHIL: I don't like the way he's glaring.

MICHELE: Henry, he's your very own son and heir. Aren't you proud?

PHIL: Evil looking bleeder.

MICHELE: He's a lovely baby. Ogy ogy.

GREG: Waa waa.

(GREG throws the teddy bear out of the pram. MICHELE picks up the teddy bear and gives it back to GREG. GREG snatches it, and glares at her. A pause. Then PHIL sniffs.)

PHIL: He has shitted himself. Ever since he came back from the hospital he's been lying there shitting himself.

MICHELE: All babies do their business.

PHIL: Not every ten minutes. Twenty-four hours a day. I tell you, he's a born trouble maker.

MICHELE: I don't know how you can say that of an innocent little babe.

(GREG throws the teddy bear out of the pram.)

GREG: Waa waa.

PHIL: I tell you, we're going to rue the day we had that. Rue the day.

GREG: Waa waa. I'm catching on fast. My Daddy hates my

guts. I bet I was a contraceptual blunder. I bet he came home pissed, and had a faux pas with my Mum. Probably slit the rubber with his thumb nail. Waa! Waa!

(MICHELE picks up the teddy bear, and gives it to GREG. GREG looks around evilly, then tears the teddy bear apart piece by piece, with great deliberation. When he's only got the head left, there's a pause.)

PHIL: He's a monster.

(GREG pokes the teddy bear's eye out with his fingers, throws the head away, and makes baby noises of delight.)

GREG: Gug gug gug.

PHIL: You've gone and given birth to a monster. I knew he was a monster at his christening, when he sicked up in the font. Remember what the vicar said. God Help Us!

MICHELE: Don't talk like that Henry.

PHIL: He's got an evil mind! Three weeks old and already mutilating. What's he gonna be like when he's thirty? A Frankenstein! A new Hitler! Mind you he gets it from your side. I always said your mother was half cut.

MICHELE: Don't talk like that. He's beautiful.

(GREG puts his tongue out at PHIL.)

PHIL: He'll have to go! We'll parcel him up. In newspaper. Dump him at the gates of Buckingham Palace.

MICHELE: You never wanted a little one. Did you?

PHIL: He's one big accident.

MICHELE: Your own son, unwanted by you.

PHIL: One big mistake.

MICHELE: And whose?

(A pause.)

PHIL: I knew you'd bring that up. I knew you'd bring that up.

MICHELE: You no good lower class lout.

PHIL: Bringing it all up aren't you.

MICHELE: I am. I will. From now on till your dying day. You had your fun.

PHIL: My conjugal right weren't it? Fun.

MICHELE: And now you pay the price. Him!

(GREG gives PHIL a 'V' sign. PHIL is suddenly tired.)

PHIL: Oh, go and change his nappies.

MICHELE: Don't you worry my lovely. He'll not dump you at any palace door.

(MICHELE wheels GREG off. PHIL is left standing there.)

SCENE THREE: ON BRIDLINGTON'S SAND

PHIL: I fumbled, that's all. Every man does, from time to time. Fumble.

(He protests.)

I was young! A randy blighter! Ethel was a fun-loving chick. And not a care had either of us. We married blithely, in a smoochy mood. It were all roses, and kisses, and a lover's moon, and Frank Sinatra singing 'Strangers In The Night'.

(A pause.)

But a few years on, and she got varicose veins. False teeth. Bunions the size of oranges. And she started going on about a kid. That she were fast getting by the age for bunning up.

(He begins to roll up his trousers to the knees.)

But I didn't want a kid. The joys of fatherhood I saw as a pain in the neck. Eagerly to be avoided. In my mind I was still a randy blighter. In my mind.

(When he has rolled his trousers up, he pauses for a few of his words, then lays the sheet carefully out in front of him, smoothing the wrinkles.)

She gave up precautions herself, Saying if nature's course was to be stopped, I was to do it. And I... fumbled.

(He sits down, facing the sheet.)

He leads us a terrible life. I've given up. I just do what the little cunt says. He said he wanted to go to the seaside. That's why we're here. On Bridlington sands.

(PHIL takes the edge of the sheet and slowly flicks it, making a wave effect. MICHELE comes on as the mother, who's raddled and weary now. She leads GREG as Skinny by the hand. He carries a bucket and spade.)

GREG: Oh look! A silly crab.

(GREG stamps on it.)

Oh look! A silly starfish.

(GREG stamps on it.)

Oh look! A silly...

(GREG is about to stamp on it, but withdraws.)

Jelly fish.

(At once, to PHIL.)

Dad, can I have your lighter? Burn up this silly jelly-fish.

MICHELE: Skinny, why you want to harm those creatures?

GREG: Cos they're there.

MICHELE: They've got as much right to be there as you have.

GREG: They not!

MICHELE: WHY not Skinny?

GREG: Cos I say not!

MICHELE: Oh dear.

(PHIL wearily.)

PHIL: Having the time of his life, is he? Beats me why he wanted to come to the bleeding seaside. Screamed his head off about it for weeks. Now he's here, what does he do? Scream his head off.

GREG: Shut your cakehole fish face.

PHIL: What did you say?

GREG: I said can I have a fresh ice.

PHIL: You did not. You said...

(PHIL makes a gesture of despair.)

Oh, stuff it.

GREG: Stuff what Daddy?

MICHELE: Oh dear.

GREG: I wanna go wee wee!

MICHELE: Oh Skinny, we passed a gents back under the pier. Why didn't you say so then?

GREG: Cos I didn't want to. Then.

PHIL: Better take him back Ethel.

GREG: I wanna go wee wee...

(GREG points at the sheet.)

In the sea!

PHIL: You cannot wee wee in the sea.

GREG: Why not!

PHIL: Cos, you horrible little boy, that is a contra-
vention of the local byelaws relating to public hygiene.

GREG: In the sea! In the sea!

MICHELE: Better let him, Henry.

PHIL: Oh all right. Let him poison the coastline. Let
thousands of bathers perish. I don't care. Anything for
peace and quiet.

GREG: Goody goody goody.

(GREG 'wades in'.)

Look at the animal!

MICHELE: What we going to do with him, Henry?

PHIL: I don't know, Ethel.

(GREG is 'in the sea', that is he has the sheet around
him, and he's sitting down with his legs out straight.)

GREG: Look at 'em, two old boots on the seashore. I know
what they're thinking. They're thinking they've just
about had enough.

PHIL: I've just about had enough, Ethel.

MICHELE: I know, Henry. But what we going to do.

GREG: An' I bet, I bet they're getting round to thinking
of putting me away.

PHIL: I'm getting round to thinking of putting him away.

GREG: Ha! They don't know even in the womb, I heard
'em. I caught on EARLY.

PHIL: He may be simple. He may be a bloody genius. But
either way he's a little sod, and I can't cope.

MICHELE: I can't cope.

PHIL: Neither of us can.

MICHELE: No.

PHIL: Cope.

(A pause.)

PHIL: They have...

(A pause.)

Places for 'em.

GREG: They want to put me in a place with nuts! But they won't get away with it. They don't know I GOT A PLAN.

(GREG goes on his back, and wriggles under the sheet, waving his arms.)

Mummy, Mummy, help.

MICHELE: It's Skinny!

GREG: Mummy, help.

MICHELE: He's drowning!

PHIL: He's having you on.

GREG: I'm drowning Mummy.

MICHELE: He is! I'm coming, my one and only!

(MICHELE 'swims' to GREG. GREG suddenly appears from under the sheet, and grabs her neck.)

GREG: You going to put Skinny away, Mummy?

MICHELE: Skinny let go of my neck!

GREG: Put Skinny away?

MICHELE: You're so heavy Skinny. OH...

(MICHELE disappears under the sheet. She makes muffled bubble noises.)

GREG: Daddy, Mummy's drowning.

PHIL: Oh my God! Hold on Ethel, my one true love!

(PHIL 'swims' to GREG. GREG suddenly grabs his neck.)

GREG: Going to put Skinny away, Daddy?

PHIL: Let go my neck you great freak!

(PHIL disappears under the sheet, joins MICHELE in muffled bubbles and cries of 'Skinny'. GREG 'swims ashore.' No more sound or movement from under the sheet.)

GREG: I drowned my Mum and Dad, and now I'm free!

(The lights begin to fade.)

And I'll kill off all the other Mums and Dads. No more fathers, beating up their kids! No more mothers, screeching! All over the age of ten, I'll kill off too.

And the world will be all PLAY. And everyone will pee in the sea, whenever they want.

(The lights are very nearly out.)

SCENE FOUR: AT MAJOR BUGGERY'S ORPHANAGE

The light is very low. GREG continuing his speech.

GREG: That were my plan. Be Dictator Of The World! But it didn't work out. An' they put me in an orphanage.

(At once the lights slam up, a bell clangs, PHIL comes out from under the sheet as The Major, zipping up his flies, MICHELE comes out from under the sheet smoothing her skirt down.)

MICHELE: Oh! Major!

PHIL: Run along Matron.

MICHELE: Yes Major.

PHIL: Major Bertram Buggery signing on. Head Warden, Queen Elizabeth Home For Orphaned Little Bleeders. Trouble with nippers is, they've all got their minds on it. And I got to get their minds off it. And my recipe is, cold porridge for breakfast, cold toast for tea, and cold showers morning noon and night. That's what made me the man I am, Gad.

(PHIL clutches his leg.)

Oh my bally leg.

(MICHELE comes forward, dragging GREG by the arm.)

MICHELE: Come on Skinny Spew. You're going to see the Major.

(MICHELE mimes going to the door, and knocking.)

The new boy, Major.

(MICHELE shoves GREG through the 'door'. A pause. Then GREG rushes forward and kicks PHIL's bad leg and makes a getaway.)

PHIL: Trod on me gouty leg, the dirty little hun! Dial 999!

(MICHELE mimes dialing a telephone.)

GREG: Kicked the old git. Dived through the window. Hid in the grounds. Waited until dark, then made it to the by-pass.

SCENE FIVE: BY-PASS

GREG thumbing a lift. PHIL, as a car and its driver, passes him, screeches to a halt, and reverses back. PHIL mimes opening the passenger's door.

PHIL: And what's a little man like you doing all alone?

GREG: I wanna go to London.

PHIL: Ooo. Know your own mind, don't you.

GREG: I'm going to burn down the Houses of Parliament.

PHIL: Ooo.

GREG: And rule the World.

PHIL: You better jump in, then.

> (They drive a few yards. Then GREG sprawls into the centre, as if thrown from the car. PHIL steps aside.)

GREG: And the man in the car, went funny. And left me in a wood.

> (PHIL does a creepy owl whistle.)

GREG: And this big police lady, with a big police dog, she got me.

> (PHIL goes down on all fours as savage police dog advancing on the scene. MICHELE as a horrid police-woman, holding the dog back. From here the lights begin to fade to the end.)

MICHELE: Where are yer? He can smell yer, so can I yer sniveller.

> (PHIL barks.)

GREG: An' they all got me. The dogs. The coppers. And Major Buggery an' the Matron. An' the old queen on the by-pass. An' they all got me, an' got at me, cos they couldn't let me grow. What I was. The Mums and Dads, could not let me grow.

> (From here GREG slowly recoils, wrapping the sheet around him. PHIL and MICHELE speak with their own voices over him, quiet, deadly, kind.)

MICHELE: You bad boy. You need education.

PHIL: Bad boy.

MICHELE: We know you're bad.

PHIL: Because we're better than you.

MICHELE: So eat up your food.

PHIL: Don't slop it now.

MICHELE: Say your prayers.

PHIL: Don't mumble them now.

MICHELE: Do your sums.

PHIL: Get them right now.

MICHELE: Learn all the letters of the alphabet.

PHIL: And be good.

MICHELE: Be good.

(From under the sheet GREG makes gug-gug, baby like sounds. He's regressed. A tape of a real baby really crying drowns him, and the fading light reaches blackout. End play.)